Vegetaria
meals

To my children, Nicholas, Lara and Scarlett

Vegetarian meals

Delicious, nutritious recipes for veggie kids

annabel karmel

1 3 5 7 9 10 8 6 4 2

The Random House Group Limited Reg. No. 954009

A CIP catalogue record for this book is available from the British Library

ISBN: 978-009-195584-7

Printed in Hong Kong

Eddison•Sadd Editions
CREATIVE DIRECTOR Nick Eddison   INDEXER Dorothy Frame
SENIOR EDITOR Katie Golsby   DESIGNER Brazzle Atkins
PROOFREADER Nikky Twyman   ILLUSTRATIONS Nadine Wikenden
PRODUCTION Sarah Rooney
COVER PHOTOGRAPHY Dave King

Notes on the text:
- For fan-assisted ovens, reduce the temperature by 20°C
- All black pepper is freshly ground • All eggs are free range
- All Cheddar cheese is suitable for vegetarians.

Contents

Introduction 6

 Breakfast 14

 Soups & snacks 24

Pasta 40

 Rice & grains 53

 Vegetables 61

Dessert 75

Index 94

 About the author • Acknowledgements 95

Introduction

Having a baby can often lead to a lifestyle reassessment. For many, this includes questioning the suitability of a vegetarian diet for their growing family. However, there is plenty of evidence to suggest that a vegetarian diet is not only safe for children, but also has many health benefits.

Studies have found that vegetarians have a lower incidence of obesity, heart disease, high blood pressure and type 2 diabetes than meat eaters. A balanced vegetarian diet is likely to exceed the recommended minimum intake of fruit and vegetables, which is linked to lower rates of some cancers.

What is a vegetarian?
Non-meat eaters come in several different guises, as follows:

Pescetarian Excludes meat and poultry; eats dairy, eggs and fish.

Lacto-ovo-vegetarian Excludes meat, poultry and fish; eats eggs (usually free-range) and dairy products. This is the most popular type of vegetarian.

Lacto-vegetarian Excludes meat, fish, poultry and eggs; eats dairy products.

Vegan Avoids eating or using all animal products.

Meeting nutritional needs
Vegetarians need to get the nutrients usually associated with meat, poultry, fish and seafood from other sources. There is sometimes unnecessary concern that a vegetarian diet will be low in nutrients found in meat and fish, such as protein, iron, calcium, zinc, vitamin B12 and vitamin D. In fact, these nutrients are found in other foods, but it's a good idea to make sure you're familiar with the best sources, so that your family gets a regular supply of all vitamins and minerals.

Iron and zinc
Iron and zinc are found in leafy green vegetables, wholegrain cereals, nuts, seeds, pulses, fruit, eggs and dairy products. However, they're more readily absorbed by the body if eaten alongside food containing vitamin C. Citrus fruits, berries and many vegetables are great sources of vitamin C, so you could combine wholegrain cereal with chopped fruit, or add broccoli or peppers to a lentil pie (*see page 70*).

Protein
Proteins are made up of amino acids, most of which we need to get from our food. Meat and fish contain some of the most readily available sources of these important nutrients, so, if you're a vegetarian, you'll need to look elsewhere. Dairy products are a useful source; you can also combine proteins from plant sources, such as grains, pulses, nuts and tofu. For example, baked beans on wholegrain toast is a good source of protein, as is houmous and wholemeal pitta bread, or my Tofu Stir-fry (*see page 67*), which is delicious!

Essential fatty acids
These are composed of two varieties – omega 6 and omega 3 – and, as with amino acids, these need to come from our diet. Oily fish is one of the best sources of omega 3; however, if you don't eat fish, you can get omega 3 from linseeds, walnut oil, leafy green vegetables and certain grains. Omega 6 is found in vegetables, nuts and seeds. It's important to have a balanced supply of both types.

Calcium
Dairy products provide a good source of calcium. If you don't eat dairy, good plant sources of calcium include leafy green vegetables

(spring greens, broccoli, parsley), fortified foods such as soya milk, tofu, dried apricots, almonds, and sesame and sunflower seeds.

Vitamin B12
This is essential for energy production and maintaining a healthy nervous system. Vitamin B12 is mostly found in meat, poultry, fish, eggs and dairy products, but is also contained in some fortified cereals, soya milk and soya protein.

Raising healthy kids the veggie way
It may seem as though feeding a vegetarian child a well-balanced diet requires a degree in Nutrition, but the basics are easy to grasp – this book is the perfect starting point. The recipes included here are great for meat-eating families, too, as they offer easy, tasty ways to get children eating their five-a-day.

Each recipe has been especially designed with youngsters in mind, as an adult vegetarian's dietary needs differ from those of a child. Vegetarian meals designed for adults are likely to be too bulky and high in fibre, and, if eaten by children, will fill them up before they're able to take on all the nutrients they need. Too much fibre can also deplete the body of important minerals like iron.

Children have different nutritional requirements as they develop. Here is a guide to raising a growing child on a vegetarian diet:

Babies
First foods are usually made up of fruit, vegetables and cereals, but, once first tastes have been accepted, it's important to introduce foods that are rich in protein – this would usually be meat and fish. At this stage, you can start to introduce foods such as tofu or beans, making sure that they are cooked well and mashed thoroughly.

Toddlers
Iron-fortified cereals will help your child get his recommended intake of iron, without eating meat. Other good sources of iron for little ones are leafy green vegetables, eggs and dairy products. Although they still have small stomachs, toddlers are usually very active and need plenty of nutrients for growth. Provide well-balanced snacks throughout the day, such as dried and fresh fruits, vegetable sticks and yoghurts.

Children
By the time children start school, their eating habits are usually well established. Vegetarian children tend to be more nutritionally aware

than their meat-eating counterparts, which will stand them in good stead for a healthy future.

Most schools now offer good vegetarian meals, but a packed lunch is a great option if your child has particular favourites. You'll find lots of lunchbox-friendly recipes in this book, such as Vegetable Tortilla Wraps (*see page 36*) and Tomato and Mozzarella Salad (*see page 39*).

As your child grows up, she'll naturally want to experiment with food. Serving healthy meals at home will ensure that she's eating well – whatever she eats when she's out of the house. Older children tend to have big appetites, so make sure you have plenty of healthy snacks to hand.

Recipe information

The recipes in this book are accompanied by helpful information on preparation and cooking times, how many portions the recipe makes and whether it's suitable for freezing. Preparation times and portion quantities should be used as a guide only, as these will vary.

Common questions
Parents often ask me about keeping their family happy and healthy on a vegetarian diet. Here are some of the most frequently asked questions, along with my answers.

Is it acceptable to raise babies and children on a vegetarian diet?
If you're raising your child on a meat-free diet, he'll need two or three portions of vegetable protein or nuts every day, to ensure that he's getting enough protein and iron.

Don't give nuts to children under one year of age. For young children, grind finely. You'll also need to make sure he gets enough calcium and vitamin B12 (*see pages 8–9*) and vitamin D (found in eggs and fortified cereals).

What are the health benefits of a vegetarian diet?
A vegetarian diet can be very healthy, but your diet won't *automatically* be healthier just because you cut out meat. Vegetarians – like meat eaters – must make sure they eat a balanced diet that includes:

- plenty of fruit and vegetables (at least five portions a day)
- plenty of potatoes, bread, rice, pasta and other starchy foods (choosing brown or wholegrain varieties where possible)
- some milk and other dairy products
- some eggs, beans and other non-dairy sources of protein
- a small amount of foods and drinks that are high in fat and sugar

Do vegetarians need vitamin supplements?
With good planning and an understanding of what constitutes a healthy, balanced vegetarian diet, you can give your child all the nutrients her body needs without the need for supplements.

Is it healthier to eat organic fruit and vegetables?
Vitamin and mineral levels in food vary depending on the soil the plants were grown in, when they were picked and how they were stored. There's no scientific evidence to suggest that organic food is healthier than non-organic.

Eating organic food is a personal choice – often made because of the environmental benefits. It's important to eat plenty of fruit and vegetables, whether or not they're organic.

Breakfast

Special scrambled eggs

Beat the eggs with the milk, and season well. Melt a little butter in a frying pan, then add the eggs, stirring until scrambled.

Melt another knob of butter in a separate pan. Add the courgettes and fry until lightly golden. Stir in the tomato and chives, then season to taste.

Gently mix the vegetables with the egg, and sprinkle over the cheese.

- 10 MINUTES
- 10 MINUTES
- 2 PORTIONS
- NOT SUITABLE FOR FREEZING

4 eggs
4 tablespoons milk
salt and pepper
2 knobs of butter
1 small courgette, topped and tailed, and chopped
1 tomato, deseeded and chopped
1 tablespoon chopped chives
2 tablespoons finely grated Parmesan-style or Cheddar cheese

Eggs are packed with amino acids and minerals, and, with the exception of vitamin C, they contain every vitamin that we need. They're especially useful as a source of vitamin D, which children can be deficient in due to lack of sunshine. Eggs also contain the nutrient choline, which helps with brain development.

Toast toppings

🔪 5 MINUTES

🍳 6–8 MINUTES

🍽 2 PORTIONS

❄ NOT SUITABLE FOR FREEZING

2 tablespoons milk
75 g (3 oz) Cheddar cheese,
    grated
2–3 drops of vegetarian
    Worcestershire sauce
1 egg yolk (from a large egg)
2 slices of toast, unbuttered

Welsh rarebit

Put the milk in a small saucepan and heat gently. Add 25 g (1 oz) of the cheese and stir until melted. Repeat with another 25 g of cheese, then again with the remaining cheese. Remove from the heat, then stir in the Worcestershire sauce. Leave to cool to room temperature, then stir in the egg yolk.

Preheat the grill to High, and set the rack one shelf lower than the usual position. Spread the cheese mixture thinly over the toast, and grill for 1–2 minutes, until the cheese is puffed and golden. Watch carefully, as the egg causes the cheese to turn brown very quickly. Serve immediately.

🔪 5 MINUTES

🍳 2 MINUTES

🍽 1 PORTION

❄ NOT SUITABLE FOR FREEZING

1 tomato, thinly sliced (and
    skinned, if you wish)
1 slice of toast, lightly
    buttered
freshly ground black pepper
45 g (1½ oz) Cheddar cheese,
    grated

Tomato and cheese

Preheat the grill to High. Lay the tomato on the toast so that it overhangs the crust slightly, to prevent the crust from burning. Season with a little pepper. Evenly scatter the cheese on top. Grill for 1½–2 minutes, until the cheese is bubbling and golden. You could spread a little Marmite on the toast when you butter it, before you put the tomato on top.

Some brands of Worcestershire sauce contain anchovies. However, vegetarian and vegan versions are available in health food stores.

Best-ever banana bread

🔪 20 MINUTES

⊡ 1 HOUR

🎨 8 SLICES

❄️ SUITABLE FOR FREEZING

100 g (3½ oz) butter
100 g (3½ oz) brown sugar
1 egg
450 g (1 lb) bananas, peeled
and mashed
3 tablespoons natural
yoghurt
1 teaspoon vanilla essence
225 g (8 oz) plain flour
1 teaspoon bicarbonate of
soda
1 teaspoon ground
cinnamon
¼ teaspoon salt
100 g (3½ oz) raisins
40 g (1½ oz) pecan nuts
or walnuts, chopped
(optional)

Preheat the oven to 180°C/350°F/Gas 4. Grease and line a loaf tin measuring 22 x 11 x 7 cm (8½ x 4¼ x 2¾ in).

Beat the butter and sugar together until creamy, then add the egg and continue to beat until smooth. Add the banana, yoghurt and vanilla.

Sift together the flour, bicarbonate of soda, cinnamon and salt, and gradually beat this into the banana mixture. Finally, stir in the raisins and nuts (if using).

Bake for about 1 hour, or until a cocktail stick inserted into the centre comes out clean.

As well as making a great breakfast, this banana bread is ideal for the lunchbox.

If you child isn't keen on nuts – or has a nut allergy – you can omit them from this recipe.

Cream cheese, banana and honey wrap

Warm the tortilla in a microwave for 20 seconds on High.

Mix together the cream cheese and honey and spread over half of the tortilla. It will melt slightly, as the tortilla is warm. Arrange the slices of banana on top and roll up.

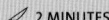 2 MINUTES

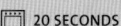 20 SECONDS

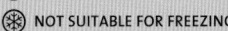 1 PORTION

NOT SUITABLE FOR FREEZING

1 flour tortilla
25 g (1 oz) cream cheese
½ teaspoon runny honey or
  1 teaspoon Dulce de Leche
1 small banana, peeled and
  sliced

Dulce de Leche is a delicious caramel spread that you can buy in most supermarkets. It's wonderful mixed with the cream cheese.

Fruity home-made muesli

Soak the porridge oats, wheatgerm and dried fruit in the fruit juice for at least 20 minutes, or overnight.

Stir in the apple and your chosen fresh fruit before serving.

🔪 10 MINUTES, PLUS 20 MINUTES FOR SOAKING

🍪 4 PORTIONS

❄ NOT SUITABLE FOR FREEZING

150 g (5 oz) porridge oats
50 g (2 oz) toasted wheat germ
25 g (1 oz) semi-dried mango, finely chopped
25 g (1 oz) dried apricots, finely chopped
25 g (1 oz) raisins
375 ml (13 fl oz) apple and mango or apple juice
1 apple, peeled, cored and grated
fresh fruit, such as strawberries, raspberries and peaches, to serve

Many of the breakfast cereals designed specifically for children are very high in sugar and low in nutrients. This delicious muesli makes a nutritious alternative. There are many fruit juices available that can be used to soak and flavour the grains. You can vary the fresh fruit you use depending on the season.

Sunshine smoothie

🔪 5 MINUTES

🥛 1 GLASS

❄️ NOT SUITABLE FOR FREEZING

1 medium banana, peeled
  and cut into chunks
½ large mango, peeled,
  stoned and cubed
1 teaspoon clear honey
120 ml (4 fl oz) pineapple
  juice
60 ml (2 fl oz) orange juice

Put the banana, mango and honey into a blender and whiz for 1–2 minutes, until smooth. Add the pineapple juice and orange juice, and whiz again until frothy.

Pour into a glass to serve.

This smoothie is a great way to use up slightly overripe bananas – the ones with brown spots that children refuse to eat.

Soups & snacks

Mediterranean tomato soup

Heat the olive oil and butter in a large saucepan and sauté the onion, carrot and celery for about 3 minutes. Add the garlic and herbs and cook for another 6 minutes. Add the tinned tomatoes and simmer over a low heat for about 15 minutes.

Stir in the tomato purée and gradually add the stock. Simmer over a medium heat for 15 minutes.

Remove the bay leaf, then transfer the soup to a food processor or blender, and whiz until smooth. Season to taste, then serve.

Onions are thought to help lower blood cholesterol and to contain substances that help prevent the blood from clotting.

🔪 15 MINUTES
🗔 40 MINUTES
🍽 6 PORTIONS
❄ SUITABLE FOR FREEZING

1 tablespoon olive oil
25 g (1 oz) butter
2 medium onions, peeled and chopped
2 medium carrots, peeled and chopped
1 stick celery, chopped
1 garlic clove, crushed
1½ tablespoons roughly chopped basil
1½ tablespoons roughly chopped tarragon
1 bay leaf
800 g (28 oz) tinned chopped tomatoes
1 tablespoon tomato purée
600 ml (1 pint) vegetable stock
salt and pepper

Sweet potato and butternut squash soup with cheesy croutons

⟋ 20 MINUTES

▭ 25 MINUTES

◔ 4 PORTIONS

❋ SUITABLE FOR FREEZING

2 tablespoons olive oil
1 small onion, peeled and
  chopped
½ teaspoon grated ginger
200 g (7 oz) butternut
  squash, peeled, deseeded
  and chopped
150 g (5 oz) sweet potato,
  peeled and chopped
450 ml (¾ pint) vegetable
  stock

Croutons
2 slices white bread
a little olive oil
2 tablespoons finely grated
  Parmesan-style cheese
a star-shaped cookie cutter

Heat the oil in a saucepan, then add the onion and ginger, and fry for 3 minutes. Add the butternut squash and sweet potato, and fry for 2 minutes. Add the stock and bring to the boil, then reduce the heat and simmer for 15 minutes. Whiz using an electric hand blender, until smooth.

Preheat the grill to High. To make the croutons, stamp 4 star shapes out of the white bread using your cookie cutter. Lightly brush them with a little oil and sprinkle with the cheese. Lay the croutons on a baking sheet and grill for 2–3 minutes, until lightly golden. Serve on top of the soup.

Parmesan cheese is made using animal rennet, and therefore isn't suitable for vegetarians. However, Parmesan-style hard cheeses that are suitable for vegetarians are available in some supermarkets and health food stores.

Golden lentil and vegetable soup

🔪 20 MINUTES

📺 30–35 MINUTES

🍪 6 PORTIONS

❄️ SUITABLE FOR FREEZING

2 tablespoons olive oil
1 onion, peeled and chopped
1 garlic clove, crushed
2 medium carrots, peeled and chopped
100 g (3½ oz) butternut squash, peeled, deseeded and chopped
100 g (3½ oz) sweet potato, peeled and chopped
200 g (7 oz) celery, sliced
50 ml (2 fl oz) water
100 g (3½ oz) red lentils
700 ml (24 fl oz) vegetable stock
1 bay leaf
1 sprig of thyme
½ teaspoon salt and pepper

Heat the oil in a fairly large saucepan, then add the onion, garlic and vegetables. Pour over the water, cover, and cook over a low heat, stirring occasionally, for 15–20 minutes, or until the vegetables are softened.

Add the lentils to the pan with the stock, bay leaf, thyme and seasoning. Simmer for 15 minutes, or until the lentils are cooked. Remove the bay leaf and thyme, then blitz the soup in a food processor. Adjust the seasoning to taste.

To save time, you can buy peeled and chopped butternut squash.

Carrot and coriander soup

Melt the butter in a saucepan. Add the onion, celery and carrots, and fry for 5 minutes. Add the ground coriander and flour, then blend in the stock. Bring to the boil, then reduce the heat and simmer for 15 minutes, until the vegetables are softened.

Whiz the soup using an electric hand blender, until smooth. Season to taste, and add the crème fraîche, to serve.

🔪 10 MINUTES
🍳 25 MINUTES
🕐 4–6 PORTIONS
❄ SUITABLE FOR FREEZING

a knob of butter
1 onion, peeled and sliced
2 sticks celery, sliced
450 g (1 lb) carrots, peeled and sliced
1½ teaspoons ground coriander
1 tablespoon plain flour
500 ml (17 fl oz) vegetable stock
salt and pepper
2 tablespoons crème fraîche

Carrots are rich in antioxidants, particularly betacarotene, which the body converts into vitamin A. Carrots have a higher concentration of antioxidants when they're cooked. It's especially important to eat the skin, as this is where most of the nutrients lie.

Mini cheese soufflés

Preheat the oven to 220°C/430°F/Gas 7. Put a baking sheet in the hot oven. Lightly grease four large ramekins (about 10 cm/4 in in diameter) or six smaller ones.

Melt the butter in a saucepan, then add the flour. Stir over the heat for a few seconds, then blend in the milk, whisking until smooth and thickened. Remove from the heat and add the mustard and cheeses. Stir until melted, then add the egg yolks and seasoning.

Put the egg whites into a food mixer and whisk until they form stiff peaks. Fold 1 tablespoon of the egg whites into the cheese mixture to loosen the consistency, then fold in the remaining egg whites and spoon into the ramekins.

Place the ramekins on the hot baking sheet, and bake for 12 minutes if you're using small ramekins or 15 minutes for larger ones. The soufflés should be well risen and lightly golden on top. Serve immediately.

15 MINUTES

15–20 MINUTES

4–6 PORTIONS

NOT SUITABLE FOR FREEZING

40 g (1½ oz) butter, plus extra for greasing
40 g (1½ oz) plain flour
300 ml (½ pint) whole milk
½ teaspoon Dijon mustard
45 g (1½ oz) Parmesan-style cheese, finely grated
25 g (1 oz) mature Cheddar cheese, grated
25 g (1 oz) Gruyère cheese, grated
3 large eggs, separated
salt and pepper

English muffin pizzas

✐ 3 MINUTES

▭ 15–20 MINUTES

🍳 4 PIZZAS

❄ NOT SUITABLE FOR FREEZING

1 tablespoon olive oil
½ red onion, peeled and chopped
½ small red or yellow pepper, deseeded and diced
50 g (2 oz) courgette, topped and tailed, and diced
50 g (2 oz) chestnut mushrooms, washed and diced
1 teaspoon chopped thyme
1 teaspoon garlic purée
2 English muffins
4 tablespoons passata
1 tablespoon sun-dried tomato paste
25 g (1 oz) Cheddar cheese, grated
25 g (1 oz) vegetarian mozzarella cheese, grated

Heat the oil in a frying pan and fry the onion, pepper, courgette and mushrooms for 8 minutes, until softened and lightly golden. Add the thyme and garlic purée, and fry for 1 minute.

Slice the muffins in half and arrange on a baking sheet, cut side up.

Preheat the grill to High. Mix together the passata and sun-dried tomato paste and spread over the muffins. Spoon over the cooked vegetables, then sprinkle with the grated Cheddar and mozzarella.

Put the pizzas under the grill for 4–5 minutes, until the cheese is melted and bubbling.

If you wish, decorate with food faces (*see right*) before serving.

Split toasted English muffins make good individual pizza bases, and by topping them yourself you can sneak in some extra veggies.

Decoration
4 black olives
8 basil leaves
8 mini mozzarella balls
8 small circles of red pepper

Veggie balls

Cook the sweet potatoes in a microwave on High, for 8–10 minutes or until soft. (Alternatively, cook in an oven preheated to 200°C/400°F/Gas 6, for 45 minutes.) Cut them in half and scoop out the flesh.

While the sweet potatoes are cooking, heat 1 tablespoon of the oil in a frying pan and add the courgette, pepper, onion, carrot and garlic. Fry for about 8 minutes, until the vegetables are soft and dry. Add to the sweet potato, with the breadcrumbs and cheese.

Shape the mixture into 20 balls, then coat in flour. Heat the remaining oil in a frying pan and fry the veggie balls a few at a time, turning frequently, until lightly golden. Alternatively, you could deep-fry them.

🖊 15 MINUTES

🍳 25 MINUTES

🥘 20 BALLS

❄ SUITABLE FOR FREEZING

2 X 250 g (9 oz) sweet potatoes, scrubbed and pricked
2 tablespoons olive oil
1 medium courgette (200 g/ 7 oz), topped and tailed, and grated
½ red pepper, deseeded and finely diced
1 onion, peeled and finely chopped
75 g (3 oz) carrot, peeled and grated
1 garlic clove, crushed
100 g (3½ oz) breadcrumbs
30 g (1 oz) Parmesan-style or Cheddar cheese, grated
a little flour, for coating

Vegetable tortilla wraps

 10 MINUTES

6 MINUTES

2 WRAPS

SUITABLE FOR FREEZING

1 tablespoon olive oil
½ red onion, peeled and
  sliced
1 small courgette, topped
  and tailed, and cut into
  ribbons
½ red pepper, deseeded and
  sliced
1 teaspoon curry powder
1 garlic clove, crushed
1 tablespoon mango
  chutney
salt and pepper
2 flour tortillas
40 g (1½ oz) Cheddar cheese,
  grated

Heat the oil in a frying pan, add the onion, courgette and pepper, and fry for 2 minutes. Add the curry powder and sauté for 1 minute, then add the garlic and fry for another 30 seconds. Stir in the mango chutney, then season.

Warm the tortillas in a microwave for a few seconds, to make them more pliable. Divide the vegetables between the two tortillas and sprinkle over the cheese. Roll up and cut in half.

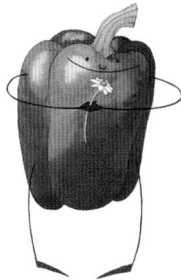

Courgettes are a good source of betacarotene, but, as most of the nutrients lie in the skin, it's best not to peel them.

Tomato and mozzarella salad

Preheat the oven to 220°C/430°F/Gas 7.

Arrange the lettuce, mozzarella and tomatoes in a bowl. Spread out the bread cubes on a baking sheet, season and drizzle over the oil. Roast in the oven for 10 minutes, until golden and crisp. Leave to cool, then add to the salad.

Mix together the dressing ingredients, and pour over the salad before serving.

5 MINUTES
10 MINUTES
4 PORTIONS
NOT SUITABLE FOR FREEZING

3 little gem lettuces, shredded
125 g (4½ oz) vegetarian mini mozzarella pearls (or 1 ball of mozzarella, cubed)
175 g (6 oz) cherry tomatoes, halved
2 slices thick-sliced white bread, cubed
salt and pepper
2 tablespoons olive oil

Dressing
4 tablespoons olive oil
1 tablespoon balsamic vinegar
1 tablespoon soy sauce
1½ teaspoons caster sugar

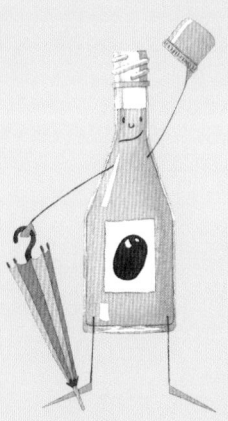

Pasta

Spaghetti with sunblush and plum tomatoes

Cook the spaghetti in a large saucepan of boiling water, according to the packet instructions.

Meanwhile, heat the olive oil in a saucepan and sauté the onion and garlic for 5–6 minutes. Add all the remaining ingredients (except for the spaghetti), cover and simmer over a low heat for 10 minutes.

Drain the spaghetti, then stir into the sauce.

10 MINUTES

20 MINUTES

4 PORTIONS

SUITABLE FOR FREEZING (SAUCE ONLY)

200 g (7 oz) spaghetti
2 tablespoons olive oil
1 onion, peeled and chopped
1 garlic clove, crushed
8 ripe plum tomatoes (about 750 g/1 lb 10 oz), skinned, deseeded and chopped
100 g (3½ oz) sunblush tomatoes
1 teaspoon balsamic vinegar
a handful of basil leaves, torn
a pinch of sugar
salt and pepper

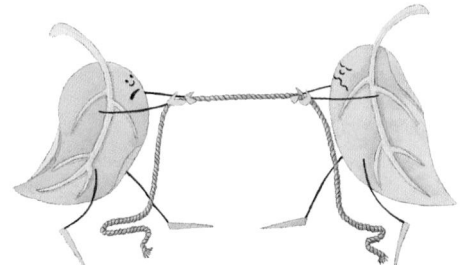

For a good flavour, you do need to use ripe tomatoes. If they're not ripe or lack flavour, add a little tomato purée.

- ✏️ 3 MINUTES
- 🍳 15–20 MINUTES
- 🍽️ 8 PORTIONS
- ❄️ SUITABLE FOR FREEZING

250 g (9 oz) spaghettini
2 tablespoons vegetable oil
1 onion, peeled and finely chopped
1 garlic clove, crushed
½–1 teaspoon grated fresh ginger
150 g (5 oz) carrots, peeled and finely diced
100 g (3½ oz) red pepper, deseeded and finely diced
150 g (5 oz) courgettes, topped and tailed, and finely diced
3 tomatoes, skinned, deseeded and chopped
4 spring onions, finely sliced
350 ml (12 fl oz) vegetable stock
2 tablespoons soy sauce
1 tablespoon vegetarian oyster sauce (*see right*)
1 tablespoon sweet chilli sauce
salt and pepper

Spaghettini with spring vegetables

Cook the spaghettini in a large saucepan of boiling water, following the packet instructions. Drain and set aside.

Heat the oil in a wok or frying pan and sauté the onion, garlic and ginger for 3 minutes, stirring occasionally. Add the carrot, red pepper and courgette, and cook, stirring occasionally, for 4 minutes. Add the tomatoes and spring onion, and cook, stirring, for 2 minutes. Pour in the stock, soy sauce, oyster sauce and sweet chilli sauce, and cook for 1 minute. Season to taste.

Drain the spaghettini and toss with the sauce. You could serve with freshly shaved Parmesan-style cheese, if you wish.

Spaghettini is very thin spaghetti, which can be found in the supermarket. You could use linguine or spaghetti if you prefer.

Vegetarian oyster sauce is made from oyster mushrooms and is available in Asian food stores.

Pasta twirls with cheese sauce and broccoli

- 5 MINUTES
- 15 MINUTES
- 2 PORTIONS
- NOT SUITABLE FOR FREEZING

125 g (4½ oz) fusilli pasta
50 g (2 oz) broccoli, cut into
   small florets
40 g (1½ oz) butter
40 g (1½ oz) plain flour
570 ml (20 fl oz) milk
a little freshly grated
   nutmeg
a pinch of cayenne pepper
50 g (2 oz) mature Cheddar
   cheese, grated
25 g (1 oz) Parmesan-style
   cheese, grated
salt and pepper

Cook the pasta following the packet instructions. Steam the broccoli florets for about 3 minutes, until tender.

Meanwhile, melt the butter in a saucepan, stir in the flour, and cook over a low heat for 1 minute. Gradually whisk in the milk, nutmeg and cayenne pepper. Bring to the boil and whisk until you have a smooth, glossy sauce, then simmer gently for 3 minutes. Whisk in the cheeses until melted, and season to taste.

Drain the pasta and mix together with the cheese sauce and broccoli.

Broccoli is king of the healthy vegetable superstars. To get the best from it, it should be steamed, as boiling almost halves its vitamin content.

Spinach and ricotta cannelloni

🔪 20 MINUTES

🔲 65–70 MINUTES

🍳 6 PORTIONS

❄️ SUITABLE FOR FREEZING

First, make the tomato sauce. Heat the oil in a saucepan, then add the onion and garlic, and fry for 3 minutes. Add the tinned tomatoes, tomato paste and water, and bring to the boil. Simmer for 15 minutes, then spoon into a shallow ovenproof dish.

To make the filling, heat the spinach and water in a pan until the spinach has wilted. Drain well, then chop. Transfer to a bowl and combine with the cheeses, egg and seasoning. Use a piping bag to pipe the mixture into the cannelloni tubes, then arrange the tubes on top of the tomato sauce.

Preheat the oven to 200°C/400°F/Gas 6, then make the cheese sauce. Melt the butter in a saucepan, add the flour and blend in the milk. Stir until thickened, then add half of the Cheddar and season with salt and pepper. Pour over the cannelloni, then sprinkle over the remaining Cheddar cheese.

Bake for 35–40 minutes, until the pasta is cooked through and the cheese is bubbling.

12 dried cannelloni tubes

Tomato sauce
1 tablespoon olive oil
1 onion, peeled and chopped
1 garlic clove, crushed
400 g (14 oz) tinned chopped tomatoes
1 tablespoon sun-dried tomato paste
200 ml (7 fl oz) water

Filling
250 g (9 oz) baby spinach
2 tablespoons water
250 g (9 oz) ricotta cheese
50 g (2 oz) Parmesan-style cheese, grated
1 egg, beaten
salt and pepper

Cheese sauce
45 g (1½ oz) butter
45 g (1½ oz) plain flour
600 ml (1 pint) milk
100 g (3½ oz) Cheddar cheese, grated

Lasagne with spinach, cheese and tomato

✎ 25 MINUTES

▦ 40 MINUTES

🍴 4 PORTIONS

❄ SUITABLE FOR FREEZING

First, make the tomato sauce. Heat the olive oil and sauté the onion and garlic until softened. Add the tomato purée and cook for 1 minute, then add all the remaining ingredients. Simmer, uncovered, for 10 minutes, then season to taste.

While the sauce is cooking, prepare the spinach and cheese layer. Melt the butter in a frying pan and sauté the spinach for 2 minutes. In a food processor, blend together the spinach, cottage cheese, egg, cream and Parmesan-style or Cheddar cheese. Season with a little black pepper.

Preheat the oven to 180°C/350°F/Gas 4. To assemble the lasagne, spread a thin layer of tomato sauce in a fairly deep ovenproof dish measuring about 23 x 15 cm (9 x 6 in), then lay 2 sheets of lasagne on top. Cover with half the spinach mixture, a third of the mozzarella and a third of the remaining tomato sauce. Repeat these layers, then cover with the remaining 2 sheets of lasagne, followed by the last of the tomato sauce and mozzarella. Finally, sprinkle the Gruyère on top. Bake in the oven for about 25 minutes.

15 g (½ oz) butter
225 g (8 oz) frozen or 450 g (1 lb) fresh spinach, cooked and thoroughly drained
175 g (6 oz) vegetarian cottage cheese
1 egg, lightly beaten
2 tablespoons double cream
25 g (1 oz) Parmesan-style or Cheddar cheese, grated
6 sheets lasagne
125 g (4½ oz) vegetarian mozzarella cheese, grated
15 g (½ oz) Gruyère cheese, grated

Tomato sauce
1 tablespoon olive oil
1 onion, peeled and chopped
1 garlic clove, crushed
2 tablespoons tomato purée
800 g (28 oz) tinned chopped tomatoes, drained
1 tablespoon chopped parsley
1 tablespoon basil leaves, torn
1 teaspoon dried oregano
½ teaspoon sugar
salt and pepper

Pappardelle with broccoli and sunblush tomatoes

/ 6 MINUTES

17–18 MINUTES

4 PORTIONS

NOT SUITABLE FOR FREEZING

2 tablespoons light olive oil
1 medium red onion, peeled and finely sliced
175 g (6 oz) broccoli florets
1 vegetable stock cube dissolved in 350 ml (12 fl oz) boiling water
60 g (2 oz) sunblush tomatoes, chopped
4 tablespoons double cream
25 g (1 oz) Parmesan-style cheese, grated, plus extra to garnish
salt and pepper
150 g (5 oz) pappardelle or tagliatelle

Heat the oil in a large pan and sauté the onion over a low heat for 10 minutes. Add the broccoli, vegetable stock and sunblush tomatoes. Reduce the heat and simmer for 7–8 minutes, stirring occasionally. Add the double cream and Parmesan-style cheese, and season with salt and pepper.

While the vegetables are cooking, cook the pasta in a large pan of lightly salted boiling water, according to the packet instructions. Drain, then toss with the broccoli and tomato sauce. Serve with extra grated Parmesan-style cheese.

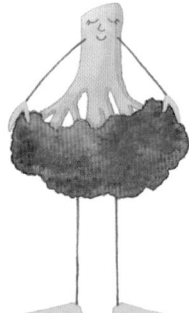

Vegetable Pad Thai

Cook the noodles in boiling salted water, according to the packet instructions. Add the broccoli for the last 3 minutes of the cooking time. Drain and refresh in cold water.

Heat the sesame oil and fry the shallots or onion, pepper, carrot and garlic for 5 minutes. Add the noodles and broccoli, along with all the ingredients for the sauce. Toss together over the heat, until heated through. Season to taste.

You could add some strips of egg (see Chinese Fried Rice on page 58), chopped peanuts or some cubes of fried tofu. You could also add a little red chilli with the shallots or onions.

Vegetarian fish sauce (or Nam Pla) is available in some Asian food stores. You could use vegetarian oyster sauce instead (see page 42).

🖊 10 MINUTES

🍳 15 MINUTES

🥘 4 PORTIONS

❄ NOT SUITABLE FOR FREEZING

175 g (6 oz) medium rice noodles
75 g (3 oz) broccoli, cut into florets
2 tablespoons sesame oil
2 shallots or 1 onion, peeled and sliced
½ red pepper, deseeded and thinly sliced
1 carrot, peeled and cut into thin strips
1 garlic clove, crushed
salt and pepper

Sauce
2 tablespoons soy sauce
1 tablespoon sweet chilli sauce
1 tablespoon vegetarian fish sauce, or 2 teaspoons hoisin sauce
1 tablespoon brown sugar

Vegetable tagliatelle

✏ 7 MINUTES

▦ 15 MINUTES

🕒 4 PORTIONS

❄ NOT SUITABLE FOR FREEZING

250 g (9 oz) tagliatelle

75 g (3 oz) broccoli, cut into florets

1 tablespoon sunflower oil

1 onion, peeled and sliced

½ red pepper, deseeded and diced

1 courgette, topped and tailed, and sliced

200 ml (7 fl oz) crème fraîche

75 ml (2½ fl oz) vegetable stock

1 tablespoon pesto

1 teaspoon lemon juice

salt and pepper

50 g (2 oz) Parmesan-style cheese, grated

Cook the tagliatelle according to the packet instructions, adding the broccoli for the last 3 minutes of the cooking time.

Meanwhile, heat the oil in a saucepan, add the onion, and fry for 3 minutes. Add the pepper and courgette, and fry until just softened.

Stir in the crème fraîche, vegetable stock and pesto, then add the pasta and broccoli. Toss together over the heat. Add the lemon juice and seasoning, then remove from the heat and stir through the Parmesan-style cheese.

Rice & grains

Jewelled couscous salad

📝 15 MINUTES

🔲 20 MINUTES

🍪 4 PORTIONS

❄️ NOT SUITABLE FOR FREEZING

180 g (6 oz) couscous
300 ml (½ pint) hot
  vegetable stock
1 red pepper, deseeded and
  diced
a bunch of spring onions,
  sliced
a bunch of parsley, chopped
50 g (2 oz) dried cranberries,
  chopped
salt and pepper
25 g (1 oz) butter
75 g (3 oz) pecan nuts
25 g (1 oz) brown sugar

Dressing

1½ tablespoons sweet
  balsamic vinegar
1 tablespoon white wine
  vinegar
1 teaspoon caster sugar
1 teaspoon Dijon mustard
6 tablespoons olive oil

Put the couscous into a bowl and pour over the stock. Stir, then cover with clingfilm and leave to soak for 20 minutes. Fluff up with a fork. Add the pepper, spring onions, parsley and cranberries, and season to taste.

Melt the butter in a small frying pan, then add the pecan nuts and sprinkle over the sugar. Cook over a fairly high heat until the nuts are caramelized. Tip out the nuts and spread them out to cool, then roughly chop.

Mix together all the dressing ingredients and pour over the couscous, then add the pecan nuts and combine.

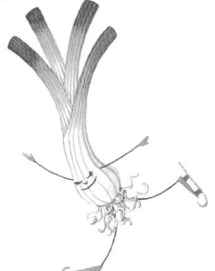

Herbs have many medicinal properties. Parsley contains vitamin C and iron, and chewing on parsley is a good breath freshener, especially after eating garlic.

Pearl barley risotto

Heat the oil in a saucepan and sauté the onion and red pepper for about 5 minutes, until softened. Add the garlic and sauté for 30 seconds, then add the pearl barley and cook for 1 minute, stirring. Pour over the stock and bring to the boil. Cover and simmer for 15 minutes, then remove the lid and simmer for another 10 minutes, or until the pearl barley is cooked and the stock has been absorbed.

Meanwhile, melt the butter in a small frying pan and sauté the mushrooms for about 3 minutes. Stir the mushrooms into the pearl barley, and season to taste.

5 MINUTES

35 MINUTES

4 PORTIONS

NOT SUITABLE FOR FREEZING

1 tablespoon olive oil
1 onion, peeled and chopped
1 red pepper, deseeded and chopped
1 garlic clove, crushed
175 g (6 oz) pearl barley
600 ml (1 pint) vegetable stock
a knob of butter
60 g (2 oz) brown cap mushrooms, roughly chopped
salt and pepper

Pearl barley is barley with all the bran removed, which gives the round, shiny grains their pearlescent white colour.

If you wish, you could leave out the mushrooms and, instead, add 50 g (2 oz) frozen peas for the last 4 minutes of the cooking time.

Baked risotto with tomato and courgette

2 tablespoons olive oil
1 medium onion, peeled
  and finely chopped
1 garlic clove, crushed
1 teaspoon ground sea salt
185 g (6½ oz) risotto rice
375 ml (13 fl oz) vegetable
  stock
400 g (14 oz) plum
  tomatoes, skinned and
  chopped, or tinned
  chopped tomatoes
250 g (9 oz) courgette,
  topped and tailed, and
  diced
65 g (2½ oz) Parmesan-style
  cheese, freshly grated
freshly ground black pepper
25 g (1 oz) butter
2 tablespoons chopped
  fresh parsley

Preheat the oven to 200°C/400°F/Gas 6. Heat the oil in a 3 litre (5 pint) capacity ovenproof dish (with a lid) over a medium heat. Sauté the onion and garlic for 5 minutes, together with the salt, until the onion is soft and translucent. Add the rice and stir over the heat for 5 minutes. Add the stock and tomatoes, and bring to simmering point, stirring occasionally. Stir in the courgette and sprinkle with 50 g (2 oz) of the Parmesan-style cheese and the black pepper, and cook for 2 minutes. Cover the dish and bake the risotto for 30 minutes, or until the rice is cooked.

Stir in the butter and remaining cheese, cover, and leave for a few minutes. Scatter the parsley over the top and serve.

It's best to serve this risotto straight away, but, if you are reheating it, add a little extra stock.

Yellow risotto

Preheat the oven to 180°C/350°F/Gas 4. Heat the oil in a casserole dish that's safe to use on the hob. Add the onion, carrots and pepper, and fry for 3–4 minutes. Add the garlic, rice and turmeric, and stir over the heat for 2 minutes. Add the hot stock, bring to the boil and cover.

Cook the risotto in the oven for 15 minutes, or until the rice is just cooked. Add the peas, cheese and crème fraîche, and stir until the cheese has melted. Season to taste.

✐ 15 MINUTES
▢ 25 MINUTES
◷ 4 PORTIONS
✳ NOT SUITABLE FOR FREEZING

2 tablespoons olive oil
1 onion, peeled and chopped
2 carrots, peeled and diced
½ red pepper, deseeded and diced
1 garlic clove, crushed
200 g (7 oz) risotto rice
¼ teaspoon turmeric
750 ml (1¼ pints) hot vegetable stock
75 g (3 oz) frozen peas, defrosted
30 g (1 oz) Parmesan-style cheese, grated
1 tablespoon crème fraîche
salt and pepper

Chinese fried rice

✎ 10 MINUTES

⬚ 20–25 MINUTES

◷ 4–6 PORTIONS

❄ NOT SUITABLE FOR FREEZING

200 g (7 oz) long grain rice
2 tablespoons sunflower oil
2 eggs
2 tablespoons soy sauce,
   plus 1 teaspoon
1 tablespoon water
2 shallots (or 1 banana
   shallot), peeled and thinly
   sliced
1 fat garlic clove, crushed
1 tablespoon soft dark
   brown sugar
¼ red pepper, deseeded and
   diced
50 g (2 oz) baby corn, cut
   into discs
100 g (3½ oz) frozen peas

Cook the rice following the packet instructions. Then drain, rinse with cold water and leave to drain again and cool.

Heat 1 tablespoon of the oil in a wok or frying pan. Beat the eggs with 1 teaspoon of the soy sauce and the water. Add to the wok and swirl the mixture around as it cooks, to make a thin omelette. When the egg is just set, flip it over and cook for a few seconds on the other side. Roll it up in the pan, then place on a chopping board and cut into thin slices.

Heat the remaining oil and stir-fry the shallots for 2–3 minutes, until starting to brown. Stir in the garlic and cook for 1 minute, then stir in the sugar and cook for 1–2 minutes, until dissolved. Add the pepper and baby corn, and cook for 3–4 minutes, until starting to soften.

Add the cooled rice and the peas, and stir-fry for 3–4 minutes, until the rice is hot and the peas have defrosted. Stir in the remaining soy sauce and omelette pieces. If you wish, you could serve with extra soy sauce.

Yummy rice with tomatoes and pesto

- 🔪 10 MINUTES
- ⬛ 10 MINUTES
- 🍽 3 PORTIONS
- ❄ NOT SUITABLE FOR FREEZING

150 g (5 oz) long grain rice
1 medium carrot, peeled and chopped
1 tablespoon sunflower oil
1 onion, peeled and chopped
1 medium courgette, topped and tailed, and diced
½ red pepper, deseeded and diced
1 garlic clove, crushed
150 ml (¼ pint) passata
2 teaspoons red pesto
1 tablespoon chopped basil
20 g (¾ oz) Parmesan-style cheese, grated
1 teaspoon balsamic vinegar

Cook the rice following the packet instructions. Add the carrot for the last 10 minutes of the cooking time (if you're using quick-cook rice, they will take the same amount of time), then drain.

Heat the oil, then fry the onion, courgette, red pepper and garlic for 5 minutes until soft. Add the passata and pesto and simmer for 2 minutes.

Add the rice and carrot to the pan, along with the basil, Parmesan-style cheese and balsamic vinegar. Stir over the heat for 30 seconds to warm through.

You could use boil-in-the-bag rice, in which case simply put the carrots into the boiling water with the bag of rice.

Vegetables

Annabel's veggie burgers

📝 20 MINUTES, PLUS 30 MINUTES FOR CHILLING

🔲 25–30 MINUTES

🍳 8 BURGERS

❄ SUITABLE FOR FREEZING

350 g (12 oz) medium potatoes, skins on
1½ tablespoons olive oil
150 g (5 oz) red onion, peeled and finely chopped
150 g (5 oz) small leeks, chopped
150 g (5 oz) carrot, peeled and grated
100 g (3½ oz) brown cap mushrooms, chopped
1 garlic clove, crushed
1 teaspoon fresh thyme leaves
1 tablespoon soy sauce
40 g (1½ oz) Gruyère cheese, grated
75 g (3 oz) fresh breadcrumbs
2 teaspoons clear honey
1 egg yolk (from a small egg)
salt and pepper
plain flour, for dusting
sunflower oil, for frying

Prick the potatoes and microwave them on High for about 10 minutes, until soft. Alternatively, boil the potatoes in a saucepan of water, with the skins on, for 30 minutes. Set aside to cool.

Meanwhile, heat the oil in a large frying pan and sauté the onion, leek, carrot, mushrooms, garlic and thyme for 10 minutes, stirring occasionally, until the vegetables are soft and dry. Leave to cool.

Peel the potatoes and lightly mash with a fork. Place in a bowl with the cold vegetables and remaining ingredients, except for the flour and oil. Mix together and season well. Shape the mixture into 8 burgers, then put them in the fridge for 30 minutes.

Lightly flour the burgers on both sides, then fry in a little sunflower oil for 3–4 minutes on each side, until cooked through and golden.

Serve in a burger bun with salad and ketchup. If you wish, you could decorate the bun to look like a rabbit (*see right*).

To freeze, place the cooked burgers on a tray lined with clingfilm. When frozen, wrap them individually in clingfilm. You can then remove from the freezer as needed.

Cashew burgers

Bring a saucepan of water to the boil and cook the sweet potato until soft, then drain.

Meanwhile, tip the cashew nuts into a blender or food processor and whiz until finely chopped. Transfer to a large mixing bowl, along with the breadcrumbs, thyme and Cheddar cheese.

Heat the oil in a frying pan and add the onion, leek, carrot and mushrooms. Fry for 10 minutes, or until soft. Then add the garlic and fry for another minute. Add the vegetables to the breadcrumb mixture, along with the sweet potato and honey. Mash together and season.

Divide the mixture into 8 portions and shape into burgers. Coat them in the flour, then fry in a little oil for 2–3 minutes on each side, until golden.

/ 20 MINUTES

📅 20 MINUTES

🍪 8 BURGERS

❋ SUITABLE FOR FREEZING

150 g (5 oz) sweet potato, peeled and chopped
50 g (2 oz) roasted cashew nuts
50 g (2 oz) white breadcrumbs
2 teaspoons chopped thyme
50 g (2 oz) Cheddar cheese, grated
1 tablespoon sunflower oil, plus extra for frying
1 red onion, peeled and chopped
½ leek, washed, peeled and chopped
1 carrot, peeled and grated
100 g (3½ oz) chestnut mushrooms, washed and roughly chopped
1 garlic clove, crushed
1 teaspoon honey
salt and pepper
a little flour, for coating

Cashew nuts are a very rich source of essential vitamins like iron and zinc. They are also a good source of antioxidants.

Tofu and vegetable burgers

- 20 MINUTES
- 15–20 MINUTES
- 8 BURGERS
- SUITABLE FOR FREEZING

100 g (3½ oz) broccoli, cut into small florets
15 g (½ oz) butter
200 g (7 oz) button mushrooms, roughly chopped
1 garlic clove, crushed
285 g (10 oz) firm tofu
100 g (3½ oz) unsalted cashew nuts
3 spring onions, finely sliced
1 medium carrot, peeled and finely grated
100 g (3½ oz) fresh breadcrumbs
1 tablespoon vegetarian oyster sauce
1 tablespoon honey
salt and pepper
plain flour, for coating
vegetable oil, for frying

Blanch the broccoli in lightly salted boiling water for 2–3 minutes, until tender.

Melt the butter in a frying pan and sauté the mushrooms and garlic for 3–4 minutes, until softened. Transfer to a food processor with the broccoli and all the other ingredients, except for the seasoning, flour and vegetable oil. Whiz until well combined, and season with salt and pepper. Form into 8 burgers, coat in flour and sauté over a medium heat, for 2–3 minutes on each side, until golden.

Tofu (also called bean curd) is made by coagulating soy juice and pressing the resultant curds into soft white blocks. Tofu is high in protein, calcium and iron, and low in saturated fats. This combination of tofu, nuts and vegetables makes these burgers very nutritious.

Tofu stir-fry

Put all the marinade ingredients into a bowl. Add the tofu and marinate for 20 minutes. Drain the tofu, reserving the marinade, and coat the tofu in the flour.

Heat 2 tablespoons of the oil in a frying pan, and fry the tofu until golden on all sides. Set aside.

Heat the remaining oil in the pan, then add the vegetables and fry for 3 minutes. Add the marinade and toss over the heat. Add the tofu and gently toss together. Serve with rice or noodles.

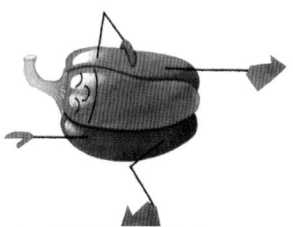

Firm tofu makes a good meat substitute in stir-fries, and is well known for its ability to absorb other flavours.

10 MINUTES, PLUS 20 MINUTES FOR MARINATING

15 MINUTES

4 PORTIONS

NOT SUITABLE FOR FREEZING

1 pack (350 g/12 oz) firm tofu, cut into cubes
50 g (2 oz) plain flour
3 tablespoons sunflower oil
1 onion, peeled and sliced
1 red pepper, deseeded and sliced
100 g (3½ oz) sugar snap peas, topped and tailed, and sliced
2 pak choi, stork removed, and sliced

Marinade

3 tablespoons soy sauce
3 tablespoons mirin
1 garlic clove, crushed
2 tablespoons sweet chilli sauce

Cheesy baked potato
1 baked potato, cut in half
100 g (3½ oz) butternut
squash, cut into chunks
and steamed until soft
¼ teaspoon Dijon mustard
10 g (¼ oz) butter
20 g (¾ oz) Cheddar
cheese, grated

Chilli baked beans
150 g (5 oz) baked beans
2 teaspoons chilli sauce
a few drops of Tabasco
2 baked potatoes
20 g (¾ oz) Cheddar
cheese, grated

Broccoli and cheese
15 g (½ oz) butter
15 g (½ oz) plain flour
150 ml (¼ pint) milk
½ teaspoon Dijon mustard
30 g (1 oz) Cheddar cheese,
grated
20 g (¾ oz) Parmesan-style
cheese, grated
125 g (4½ oz) small broccoli
florets, steamed until soft
1 baked potato

Baked potato toppings

Preheat the oven to 200°C/400°F/Gas 6. Wash and prick medium baking potatoes. Bake for 1 hour, or until tender.

Cheesy baked potato with butternut squash
Scoop out the flesh of the potato and mash with the butternut squash, mustard and butter. Season to taste. Put the mixture into the potato shells, cover with the Cheddar and grill for 5–6 minutes.

Chilli baked beans
Preheat the grill to High. Mix together the beans, chilli sauce and Tabasco. Cut a cross in the top of the potatoes, gently squeeze and spoon in the filling. Top with the cheese. Grill until bubbling.

Broccoli and cheese
Melt the butter, stir in the flour and cook for 1 minute. Remove from the heat and gradually whisk in the milk until smooth. Stir over a low heat until it comes to the boil, then cook for 1 minute – it should be quite thick. Stir in the mustard, cheeses and broccoli, and season to taste. Cut a cross in the top of the potato, gently squeeze and spoon in the filling.

Vegetable tagine

Heat the oil in a saucepan and fry the onion for 2 minutes. Add the garlic and vegetables, then the spices and curry paste, and fry for 1 minute. Add the remaining ingredients, bring to the boil, then simmer for 20 minutes, until all the vegetables are cooked. Remove the cinnamon stick. Serve with couscous.

✎ 15 MINUTES

🔲 25 MINUTES

🍳 4 PORTIONS

❄ SUITABLE FOR FREEZING

1 tablespoon sunflower oil
1 onion, peeled and chopped
2 garlic cloves, crushed
200 g (7 oz) butternut squash, peeled, deseeded and diced
150 g (5 oz) carrots, peeled and diced
1 large courgette, topped and tailed, and diced
1 teaspoon ground cumin
1 teaspoon ground coriander
2 teaspoons korma curry paste
400 g (14 oz) tinned chopped tomatoes
200 ml (7 fl oz) vegetable stock
1 cinnamon stick
1 tablespoon honey

A tagine is a kind of stew, with all the fragrant flavours of Morocco. The name comes from the traditional clay dish in which it was originally cooked.

Tasty lentil pie

✐ 15 MINUTES

▦ 35–40 MINUTES

◷ 4 PORTIONS

✻ SUITABLE FOR FREEZING

350 g (12 oz) potatoes,
   peeled and cut into 5 mm
   (¼ in) slices
1 tablespoon olive oil
1 red onion, peeled and
   chopped
½ red pepper, deseeded and
   chopped
1 small courgette, topped
   and tailed, and chopped
2 garlic cloves, crushed
75 g (3 oz) red lentils
400 g (14 oz) tinned
   chopped tomatoes
200 ml (7 fl oz) vegetable
   stock
2 teaspoons sun-dried
   tomato paste
salt and pepper
6 tablespoons double cream
50 g (2 oz) Cheddar cheese,
   grated

Cook the potatoes in boiling water for about
7 minutes, until just cooked. Preheat the oven
to 220°C/430°F/Gas 7.

Meanwhile, heat the oil in a saucepan and fry
the onion, pepper and courgette for 4 minutes. Stir
in the garlic and lentils, then add the tomatoes,
stock and sun-dried tomato paste. Bring to the
boil, cover and simmer for 15–20 minutes, or until
the lentils are cooked. Season and spoon into an
ovenproof dish.

Drain the potatoes and arrange on top of the
lentils. Pour over the cream and sprinkle with the
cheese. Bake for 15 minutes, until lightly golden
and bubbling.

*Lentils are an excellent source of protein, iron,
selenium and potassium, and are therefore an
ideal food for vegetarians.*

Vegetarian shepherd's pie

✎ 20 MINUTES

🔲 75–90 MINUTES

🕐 4–6 PORTIONS

❄ SUITABLE FOR FREEZING

1 tablespoon olive oil
1 medium red onion, peeled
  and finely chopped
1 medium carrot, peeled
  and grated
1 garlic clove, crushed
150 g (5 oz) green lentils,
  rinsed
400 g (14 oz) tinned
  chopped tomatoes
350 ml (12 fl oz) vegetable
  stock
150 ml (¼ pint) water
2 tablespoons tomato purée
1 tablespoon soy sauce
4 teaspoons brown sugar
750 g (1 lb 10 oz) potatoes,
  peeled and cut into chunks
20 g (¾ oz) butter
4 tablespoons milk
salt and pepper
1 egg, lightly beaten
50 g (2 oz) Cheddar cheese,
  grated

Heat the oil in a large saucepan and sauté the onion and carrot for 8–10 minutes, stirring occasionally, until soft and starting to brown. Add the garlic and cook for 1 minute, then stir in the lentils, tomatoes, stock, water, tomato purée, soy sauce and sugar. Bring to the boil, reduce the heat, cover and simmer for 40–45 minutes, until the lentils are soft. Add a little extra water if necessary.

Meanwhile, boil the potatoes in plenty of salted water for about 15 minutes, until just tender. Drain, then mash well. Beat in the butter and milk and season to taste.

Preheat the oven to 200°C/400°F/Gas 6. Season the lentils with pepper, then divide between 4 small baking dishes or 6 ramekins. Spread the mashed potato over the lentils and fluff up with a fork.

Put the pies on a baking sheet, brush with the egg and sprinkle with the grated cheese. Bake for 25–30 minutes, until the potato is golden on top and the pies are piping hot. Allow to cool slightly before serving.

lentil curry

Heat the oil in a saucepan, add the onion, pepper and carrot, and fry for 5 minutes. Add the garlic, spices, curry paste and lentils, then blend in the tomatoes, stock, tomato purée and mango chutney. Bring to the boil, cover and simmer for 15 minutes, or until the lentils are tender.

Season to taste and serve with rice.

✎ 10 MINUTES

▦ 25 MINUTES

◔ 6–8 PORTIONS

❄ SUITABLE FOR FREEZING

1 tablespoon sunflower oil
1 onion, peeled and chopped
½ red pepper, deseeded and diced
2 carrots, peeled and diced
1 garlic clove, crushed
1 teaspoon ginger, grated
1 teaspoon cinnamon
1 teaspoon cumin
1 teaspoon ground coriander
2 teaspoons korma curry paste
150 g (5 oz) red lentils
400 g (14 oz) tinned chopped tomatoes
500 ml (17 fl oz) vegetable stock
1 tablespoon tomato purée
2 teaspoons mango chutney
salt and pepper

Children's diets have a tendency to be rather unadventurous. Introducing children to a wide variety of flavours can prevent them from growing into fussy eaters. Mild curry is often very popular.

Vegetable tempura

vegetable oil, for frying
selection of vegetables,
   such as courgette, carrot,
   sweet potato, broccoli,
   cauliflower
ground sea salt

Tempura batter
100 g (3½ oz) plain flour
50 g (2 oz) cornflour
300 ml (½ pint) ice-cold
   sparkling water

Dipping sauce
4 tablespoons rice wine
   vinegar
1 tablespoon soft brown sugar
1 teaspoon grated fresh root
   ginger (optional)
4 tablespoons sake or rice
   wine
1 tablespoon soy sauce
1 red chilli, deseeded and
   finely sliced
1 tablespoon finely sliced
   spring onion

Preheat a deep-fat fryer to 200°C/400°F, or heat some oil in a wok or frying pan to a depth of about 7 cm (2¾ in). To check the temperature of the oil, drop in a small cube of bread. If it sizzles and turns crisp and golden, the oil is ready to use.

Mix both flours in a large bowl and, with the handle of a wooden spoon, stir in the ice-cold water until the mixture resembles double cream. Only mix lightly, as it should be quite lumpy.

Cut the courgette into batons, the carrot and sweet potato into thin strips and the broccoli and cauliflower into florets. Dip the vegetables in the batter. Deep-fry a few at a time; don't overcrowd the deep-fat fryer, or the temperature of the oil will drop. When the batter turns golden, remove from the pan using a slotted spoon, and drain on kitchen paper. Season well with sea salt.

To make the sauce, put the vinegar and sugar into a pan, bring to the boil, then simmer for 3 minutes, until reduced slightly. Add the ginger (if using) for the last minute of the cooking time. Add the sake and bring to the boil, then remove from the heat and stir in the soy sauce. Allow to cool a little, then stir in the chilli and spring onion.

Dessert

Summer puddings

Wet the insides of 4 ramekins and line them with clingfilm.

Put the sugar, blueberries and water into a saucepan, and heat until the sugar has dissolved and the blueberries are starting to soften. Add the raspberries and strawberries and simmer for about 5 minutes, until there is quite a lot of syrup.

Cut out 4 circles of bread, the same size as your ramekin bases. Dip them in the fruit syrup, then place them in the bottom of the lined ramekins. Cut the remaining bread into strips and line the sides.

Spoon the fruit into the ramekins, with as much syrup as you can fit in. Cover with clingfilm and press down. Refrigerate for 1 hour.

Turn out the puddings onto plates, remove the clingfilm and serve.

🖊 15 MINUTES

🔲 10 MINUTES

👥 4 PORTIONS

❄ NOT SUITABLE FOR FREEZING

125 g (4½ oz) caster sugar
250 g (9 oz) blueberries
3 tablespoons water
250 g (9 oz) raspberries
150 g (5 oz) strawberries, hulled and cut into small pieces
6 slices thin white bread, crusts removed

Summer berries are packed with vitamin C, which helps to strengthen the immune system and fight infection. Vitamin C also aids the absorption of iron.

Fruit compote

a knob of butter
175 g (6 oz) ripe juicy
   peaches, stoned and sliced
100 g (3½ oz) blueberries
50 g (2 oz) caster sugar
100 g (3½ oz) strawberries,
   hulled and quartered
100 g (3½ oz) raspberries
a spoonful of ice cream,
   frozen yoghurt or Greek
   yoghurt, to serve

Melt the butter in a saucepan, then add the peaches and stir gently for 30 seconds. Add the blueberries and sugar, and stir for 1 minute. Remove from the heat and add the strawberries and raspberries.

Serve with ice cream, frozen yoghurt or Greek yoghurt.

This is a great dessert to make when peaches are in season.

Peach melba pavlovas

Preheat the oven to 140°C/275°F/Gas 1. Line 2 baking sheets with non-stick baking paper.

Using an electric mixer, whisk the egg whites on full speed, adding the sugar a teaspoon at a time. Whisk until the whites are stiff and fluffy. Combine the cornflour and vinegar, then fold into the meringue.

Put a heaped tablespoon of meringue mixture onto a baking sheet, then use a teaspoon to spread into a rough 10 cm (4 in) circle. Repeat to make 8 meringues. Bake for 45 minutes to 1 hour, or until they're firm to the touch, lightly golden and come away from the paper easily. Leave to cool while you make the topping.

Combine the cream and yoghurt in a bowl. Using a blender, purée the peaches, then fold half into the cream mixture. Gently fold in the rest, to make a ripple effect. Spoon over the meringues and top with the raspberries. Garnish with a sprig of mint and a little icing sugar.

> *It's best to make these in advance and put them in the fridge, so that the cream softens the meringue.*

🔪 35 MINUTES

📅 45–60 MINUTES

🍽 4 PORTIONS

❄ NOT SUITABLE FOR FREEZING

3 egg whites (from large eggs)
175 g (6 oz) caster sugar
1 teaspoon cornflour
1 teaspoon rice wine vinegar or white vinegar

Topping
150 ml (¼ pint) double cream, stiffly whipped
6 tablespoons low-fat Greek yoghurt
400 g (14 oz) tinned sliced peaches in syrup, drained
200 g (7 oz) fresh raspberries
sprigs of mint, to garnish
icing sugar, to garnish

Brûlé-style strawberry dessert

🥄 5 MINUTES

🍽 4 PORTIONS

❄ NOT SUITABLE FOR FREEZING

150 g (5 oz) strawberries, hulled and sliced
100 g (3½ oz) blueberries
300 ml (½ pint) Greek yoghurt
4 tablespoons demerara sugar
50 g (2 oz) amaretti biscuits, crushed

Divide the strawberries and blueberries between 4 wine glasses or glass bowls. Spoon the yoghurt on top. Sprinkle over the demerara sugar and top with the crushed amaretti biscuits.

Put them in the fridge for 1 hour before serving.

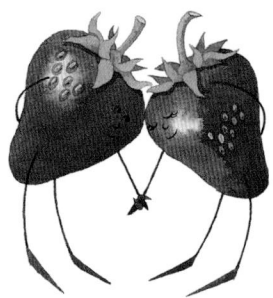

Berries are rich in vitamin C, which, when eaten at the same time, increases the absorption of iron in plant foods, such as green leafy vegetables, lentils, nuts and seeds, as well as the iron in eggs.

Crème caramel

Put 125 g (4½ oz) caster sugar into a saucepan with the water. Stir over the heat until dissolved, then let the mixture boil until it turns to a dark caramel colour. Divide between 4 ramekins. Preheat the oven to 160°C/320°F/Gas 3.

In a mixing bowl, combine the eggs, remaining sugar and vanilla. Heat the milk, then pour over the eggs and whisk everything together. Pour the mixture on top of the caramel.

Place the ramekins in a roasting tin and fill the tin with boiling water. Place it in the oven and cook for 35 minutes, until the custard has set. Allow to cool, then put the ramekins in the fridge for 4 hours.

To turn out, loosen the sides by running a small palette knife around the edges. Put a plate on top of the ramekin and turn upside down.

🖊 10 MINUTES, PLUS 4 HOURS FOR CHILLING

⬜ 45 MINUTES

🎨 4 RAMEKINS

❄ NOT SUITABLE FOR FREEZING

125 g (4½ oz) caster sugar, plus 20 g (¾ oz)
8 tablespoons water
2 eggs
1 teaspoon vanilla extract
300 ml (½ pint) milk

Apple, blackberry and raspberry crumbles

Preheat the oven to 200°C/400°F/Gas 6. Melt the butter in a saucepan, then add the apples and caster sugar. Sauté for 5 minutes, then stir in the berries. Spoon into 4 ramekins.

To make the crumble topping, rub the butter and flour together until the mixture resembles breadcrumbs. Add the sugar and salt, and stir in the pecan nuts (if using). Spoon over the fruits.

Bake for 20 minutes, until bubbling and lightly golden on top. Delicious served warm with vanilla ice cream.

10 MINUTES
25 MINUTES
4 RAMEKINS
SUITABLE FOR FREEZING

a knob of butter
2 dessert apples, peeled, cored and sliced
3 tablespoons caster sugar
150 g (5 oz) blackberries
150 g (5 oz) raspberries

Crumble topping
50 g (2 oz) cold butter, cut into pieces
100 g (3½ oz) plain flour
3 tablespoons demerara sugar
a pinch of salt
25 g (1 oz) pecan nuts, chopped (optional)

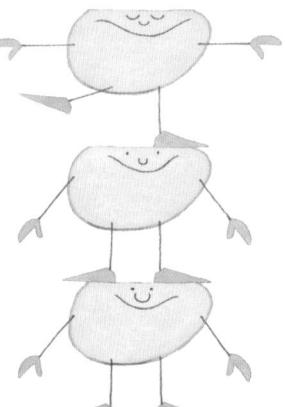

Rhubarb and strawberry crumble

15 MINUTES

25 MINUTES

6 PORTIONS

SUITABLE FOR FREEZING

25 g (1 oz) ground almonds
350 g (12 oz) rhubarb, cut
into 1 cm (⅓ in) chunks
200 g (7 oz) strawberries,
hulled and halved
75 g (3 oz) caster sugar

Crumble topping
150 g (5 oz) plain flour
a generous pinch of salt
75 g (3 oz) cold butter, cut
into pieces
85 g (3 oz) soft brown sugar
25 g (1 oz) rolled oats
50 g (2 oz) ground almonds

Preheat the oven to 200°C/400°F/Gas 6. To make the topping, mix the flour with the salt and rub in the butter using your fingertips until the mixture resembles breadcrumbs. Add the sugar and oats, and continue to rub in with your fingertips. Finally, rub in the ground almonds.

Sprinkle ground almonds over the base of a suitable ovenproof dish (a round dish with a diameter of 17 cm/6¾ in is good). This soaks up some of the juices from the fruits as they cook, to prevent the crumble from getting soggy. Mix the rhubarb and strawberries together with the sugar, and spoon into the dish.

Cover the fruit with the crumble topping and sprinkle over a little water. This will help to make the topping crispy. Bake in the oven for about 25 minutes, until the topping turns golden brown.

Annabel's peanut butter balls

Melt the peanut butter and butter in a saucepan over a low heat. In a bowl, combine the Rice Krispies and icing sugar. Pour the peanut butter mixture into the bowl and stir with a wooden spoon until combined. Using your hands, roll into 12 small balls and refrigerate for about 40 minutes.

These are good on their own, but if you want to dip the balls in chocolate, melt the chocolate in a heatproof bowl set over a pan of simmering water. Dip the balls halfway into the melted chocolate, then let the chocolate go hard – a good way to do this is to balance the balls on an ice-cube tray.

 10 MINUTES, PLUS 40 MINUTES FOR CHILLING

 5 MINUTES

 12 BALLS

 NOT SUITABLE FOR FREEZING

100 g (3½ oz) smooth peanut butter
40 g (1½ oz) butter
40 g (1½ oz) Rice Krispies
75 g (3 oz) icing sugar
75 g (3 oz) plain chocolate, broken into pieces (optional)

Peanuts contain a range of phytochemicals, which are thought to protect against heart disease and some types of cancer. Many of these phytochemicals are found in the skins, so look out for wholenut peanut butter, which contains ground-up peanut skins.

Carrot, apple and sultana muffins

 15 MINUTES

⊞ 20–22 MINUTES

🍪 12 MUFFINS

❄ SUITABLE FOR FREEZING

175 g (6 oz) self-raising flour
1 teaspoon ground ginger
1 teaspoon ground cinnamon
1 teaspoon bicarbonate of soda
100 g (3½ oz) light brown sugar
2 eggs
3 tablespoons golden syrup
150 ml (¼ pint) sunflower oil
150 g (5 oz) carrots, peeled and grated
50 g (2 oz) apple, peeled, cored and grated
75 g (3 oz) sultanas

Preheat the oven to 200°C/400°F/Gas 6. Line a muffin tin with 12 paper cases.

Sift the flour, spices and bicarbonate of soda into a bowl, then add the sugar. In a separate bowl, combine the eggs, golden syrup and oil, then pour them into the bowl with the dry ingredients. Whisk until smooth. Stir in the carrot, apple and sultanas.

Spoon the mixture into the muffin cases. Bake for 20–22 minutes, until the muffins are well risen and golden brown.

Allow the muffins to cool in the tin for about 10 minutes, then transfer to a wire rack to cool completely. Store in an airtight container.

These muffins are fun for children to make. They're perfect for lunchboxes.

Marbled chocolate cheesecake

Line the base of an 18 cm (7 in) round loose-bottomed cake tin with non-stick baking paper.

Mix the crushed biscuits with the melted butter. Spoon into the tin and smooth over, then put the tin in the fridge.

Melt the chocolate in a bowl set over a pan of simmering water. Leave to cool.

Whisk the cream cheese and cream together until thickened. Add the sugar and vanilla. Divide the mixture in half. Add the chocolate to one half of the mixture, and combine.

Remove the tin from the fridge and spread the reserved cream mixture over the biscuit base. Spoon the chocolate mixture over the top, and gently swirl the two parts together to create a marbled effect. Put the cheesecake in the fridge for 1 hour.

Remove from the tin before serving. You could decorate the top with chocolate shavings or curls if you wish.

25 MINUTES, PLUS 1 HOUR FOR CHILLING

20 MINUTES

6 SLICES

SUITABLE FOR FREEZING

150 g (5 oz) chocolate digestive biscuits, crushed
50 g (2 oz) butter, melted
200 g (7 oz) milk chocolate
150 g (5 oz) cream cheese
200 ml (7 fl oz) whipping cream
25 g (1 oz) caster –
2 teaspoons vanilla extract
chocolate shavings, to serve (optional)

Apple and almond cake

- 30 MINUTES
- 80–90 MINUTES
- 8 PORTIONS
- NOT SUITABLE FOR FREEZING

2 Granny Smith apples,
  peeled, cored and
  quartered
2 squeezes of lemon juice
175 g (6 oz) golden caster
  sugar
175 g (6 oz) unsalted butter
3 medium eggs, separated
175 g (6 oz) ground almonds
½ teaspoon almond extract
1 teaspoon baking powder,
  sifted
icing sugar, for dusting

Slice 2 of the apple quarters very thinly, put in a bowl and toss with a squeeze of lemon juice. Slice the remaining apple more thickly, put in a separate bowl and toss with more lemon juice, then sprinkle over 1 tablespoon of the sugar, toss to coat and set aside for 10 minutes.

Preheat the oven to 150°C/300°F/Gas 2. Grease a 20 cm (8 in) springform cake tin.

In a large bowl, cream the butter and remaining sugar until light and fluffy. Beat in the egg yolks, then add the almonds, almond extract and baking powder, working the mixture as little as possible.

In a clean bowl, whisk the egg whites until they form stiff peaks, then fold into the cake mixture. Add any juice from the thickly sliced apples, then pat dry with kitchen paper and gently fold into the mixture. Transfer to the prepared tin and smooth over the surface. Drain away any juice from the finely sliced apples and arrange on top of the cake. Bake for 1 hour 20 minutes to 1 hour 30 minutes, until a skewer inserted into the centre comes out clean. Run a knife around the tin to loosen the cake, then leave to cool in the tin for several hours.

Dust the cake with icing sugar before serving.

Index

Page numbers in **bold** indicate a recipe where entry is main ingredient

almonds 92
amino acids 8, 15
antioxidants 29, 65
apple juice 21
apples 21, **85**, **88**, 92
apricots 21

babies 10
baked beans **68**
balanced diet 12–13
bananas **18–19**, 22
bean curd *see* tofu
betacarotene 29, 36
biscuits **91**
blackberries **85**
blueberries **77–8**, 82
bread **16–18**, 26, **77**
breath freshener 54
broccoli 44, **48–52**, 64, **68**, 74
burgers **62–6**
   freezing 63
butternut squash **26–8**, **68–9**

cakes **91–2**
calcium 8–9, 64
carrots 25, **28–9**, 35, 42, 51, 57, **60–66**, 69, **72–4**, 88
cashew nuts **65–6**
cauliflower **74**
celery 25, **28–9**
cheese **15–16**, 19, 26, **31–2**, 39, **44–7**, 57, **60**, **68**, **91**
   Parmesan 26
children 10–11
chives 15
chocolate **87**, **91**
cholesterol 25
choline 15
coriander 29

courgettes 15, **32–6**, 42, 52, 56, **60**, **69–70**, 74
couscous 54
cranberries 54
curry 73

dairy products 8
desserts **77–92**
Dulce de Leche 19

eggs **15**, **31**, **81**, **83**
essential fatty acids 8

fish 8

iron 7, 54, 65, 66, 70, 77, 82

lacto-ovo-vegetarians 6
lacto-vegetarians 7
lasagne **45**
leeks **62–5**
lentils 28, **70–73**
lettuce **39**

mango 22
milk **83**
minerals 15
muffins **32**, **88**
mushrooms **32**, 55, **62–4**

noodles **51**
nutritional needs 7–9
nuts 12

omega oils 8
onions 25, 29, **32–6**, 42, **51–7**, **60–67**, **69–73**
   qualities 25
orange juice 22
organic food 13

pak choi **67**
parsley 54
   benefits 54
pasta **41–51**, 42
peaches 21, **78–81**

peanut butter **87**
pearl barley **55**
peas **57–8**, 67
pecan nuts 18, 54
peppers **32–6**, 42, **51–5**, **57–60**, **70**, 73
pescatarians 6
pineapple juice 22
porridge oats 21
potassium 70
potatoes **62**, **68**, **70–72**
proteins 8, 64, 70

raisins 18, 21
raspberries 21, **77–81**, 85
rhubarb **86**
rice **56–60**

selenium 70
shallots **51**, 58
soups **25–9**
spinach **45–7**
squash **26–8**, **68–9**
strawberries 21, **77–8**, 82, 86
sultanas **88**
sweet potatoes **26–8**, 35, 65, 74
sweetcorn 58

toddlers 10
tofu **66–7**
tomatoes **15–16**, 25, **39–42**, **47–8**, 56, **69–73**
tortillas 36

vegans 7
vegetables **62–74**
   see also carrots; peas; etc
vegetarians: types 6–7
vitamins 9, 13, 15, 29, 44, 54, 77, 82

walnuts 18

yogurt 82

zinc 7, 65

About Annabel Karmel

Mother of three, Annabel Karmel MBE is the UK's number one parenting author and expert on devising delicious, nutritious meals for babies, toddlers and children.

Since launching with *The Complete Baby and Toddler Meal Planner* more than two decades ago, Annabel has written 37 books, which have sold over 4 million copies worldwide, covering every stage of a child's development.

With the sole aim of helping parents give their children the very best start in life, Annabel's tried-and-tested recipes have also grown into a successful supermarket food range. From delicious Organic Baby Purées to her best-selling healthy chilled meals, these offer the goodness of a home-cooked meal for those busy days.

Annabel was awarded an MBE in 2006, in the Queen's Birthday Honours, for her outstanding work in child nutrition. She also has menus in some of the largest leisure resorts in Britain and a successful app, *Annabel's Essential Guide to Feeding Your Baby and Toddler*.

For more information and recipes, visit **www.annabelkarmel.com**.

Acknowledgements

Louise Ward and Phil Carroll (Sainsbury's Books), Fiona MacIntyre, Martin Higgins and Cat Dowlett (Ebury), Dave King (photography), Tamsin Weston (props), Kate Bliman and Maud Eden (food stylists), Lucinda McCord (recipe testing), Nick Eddison and Katie Golsby (Eddison Sadd), and Sarah Smith (PR).

annabel karmel

Other titles in the series are: